The Book Club Book Journal

SL Beaumont

Copyright © 2017 SL Beaumont

All rights reserved.

ISBN: 1542309832
ISBN-13: 978-1542309837

Paperback Writer's Publishing
Auckland, New Zealand

This Book Journal Belongs To:

The

....

Book Club

SL BEAUMONT

THE BOOK CLUB BOOK JOURNAL

Contents

Introduction i

Book Club Members 1

Book Club Rules 3

Book Club To Read List 5

Book Club's Top Books 9

Discussion Questions 11

Book Club Reading Challenges 15

Memorable Quotes 23

Book Club Reviews 25

Notes 131

SL BEAUMONT

Introduction

Welcome to the Book Club Book Journal. This Journal is intended to be used by Book Clubs everywhere to keep track of the books you've read and those that are on the 'To Read' list.

There is a page to record member contact details and your Book Club's "rules" such as how often you meet, where you meet and the process for choosing your next book.

Whether you all read the same book and then meet to discuss it or whether you read different books in rotation, then this journal will help you to keep track of all of your reading experiences.

The book review pages can be completed by one or by several readers and includes a 5-star rating system for an overall Book Club score for each book you read.

The journal includes some common Book Club questions to prompt plenty of lively discussions and several Book Club Reading Challenges to mix things up a little. So, make the tea or uncork the wine and enjoy an afternoon or evening amongst good friends and good books.

THE BOOK CLUB BOOK JOURNAL

Book Club Members

Name	Email Address	Phone #

SL BEAUMONT

Book Club Rules

Use this page to record your Book Club 'rules' (e.g. how often you meet and where, who chooses the next book etc.)

1. ....
....

2. ....
....

3. ....
....

4. ....
....

5. ....
....

6. ....
....

Or, No Rules - anything goes!

Book Club To Read List

Title	Author

THE BOOK CLUB BOOK JOURNAL

Book Club To Read List

Title	Author

THE BOOK CLUB BOOK JOURNAL

Book Club's Top Books

	Title	Author
1		
2		
3		
4		
5		
6		
7		
8		
9		
10		
11		
12		
13		
14		
15		

Discussion Questions

Some books are ideally suited to Book Clubs and include a series of discussion questions. Most however, do not. The questions below are intended to trigger ideas for your group's discussion. You only need 4-6 questions to facilitate a lively discussion, so choose and adapt as appropriate.

1. Is the story character driven or plot driven?
2. Which character did you particularly admire or dislike. What were their main character traits?
3. How does the protagonist grow or change over the course of the book?
4. What motivates different character's actions?
5. Who in the book would you most like to meet?
6. Was the plot predictable or full of twists and turns? Was it fast-paced or slow to unfold?
7. How did the book change your view on a particular event, culture or time period?
8. Was the book easy or difficult to get into? Why?
9. Would the book make a good movie? Who would you choose to play the lead character?

More Discussion Questions

10. What style is the book written in? Does it have multiple narrators or viewpoints?

11. What emotions did you feel reading the book? Were there tears? Or laughter?

12. What are the key themes of the book?

13. Do the themes of the book blend naturally with the storyline?

14. Compare or contrast with similar books that the group has read.

15. Discuss the ending. Was it expected, neatly tied up or left open for a sequel? Did it build to a satisfying conclusion?

16. Was the purpose of the book to address an issue? Was the author biased?

17. What did you learn from reading this book?

18. What do you know about the author? Would you read another book by this author?

19. Was there a specific passage or part of the book which left an impression?

20. Did this book broaden your perspective or expose you to new ideas?

Book Club Reading Challenges

Reading Challenges are a great way to break out of a rut or to supplement your reading. The following challenges have been designed as one book per month. Try one or design your own on page 21.

<u>Reading Challenge #1</u>

1. Read a classic
2. Read a Young Adult novel
3. Read a poetry collection or anthology
4. Read a biography or autobiography
5. Read a sci-fi novel
6. Read a non-fiction work
7. Read a graphic novel
8. Read a paranormal or fantasy novel
9. Read a Scandinavian crime novel
10. Read historical fiction
11. Read a comedy novel or memoir
12. Read a book by an indie author

More Book Club Reading Challenges

<u>Reading Challenge #2</u>:

1. Read a Pulitzer or Man Booker Prize winning novel
2. Read a self-improvement book
3. Read a book that has been banned at some point
4. Read a zombie novel
5. Read the first book in a new series
6. Read a book of essays or short stories
7. Read a dystopian or post-apocalyptic novel
8. Read a book that's becoming a movie this year
9. Re-read your best childhood book
10. Read a book translated into English
11. Read a horror novel
12. Read a book set in a culture you're not familiar with.

More Book Club Reading Challenges

<u>Other Reading Challenges:</u>

1. Read the World Challenge #1
   (read 12 books set in 12 different countries)

2. Read the World Challenge #2
   (read 12 books written by authors of 12 different nationalities)

3. A Series Challenge
   (choose a complete series to read)

4. A Genre Challenge
   (read 12 books from four genres that you don't normally read)

5. Classics Challenge
   (read 12 classic novels)

6. Biography Challenge
   (read 12 biographies, autobiographies or memoirs)

As you can see, the possibilities are endless. Turn over to design your own.

Book Club Reading Challenge

Design your own book club reading challenge:

	Genre, title or type of book
1	
2	
3	
4	
5	
6	
7	
8	
9	
10	
11	
12	

Memorable Quotes

Quote:
....
....
....
....
Author: ....

Quote:
....
....
....
....
Author: ....

Quote:
....
....
....
....
Author: ....

Book Club Reviews

Use the next three pages to index your reviews.

#	Title	Date	Page
1			31
2			33
3			35
4			37
5			39
6			41
7			43
8			45
9			47
10			49
11			51
12			53
13			55
14			57
15			59
16			61

Book Club Reviews

#	Title	Date	Page
17			63
18			65
19			67
20			69
21			71
22			73
23			75
24			77
25			79
26			81
27			83
28			85
29			87
30			89
31			91
32			93
33			95

Book Club Reviews

#	Title	Date	Page
34			97
35			99
36			101
37			103
38			105
39			107
40			109
41			111
42			113
43			115
44			117
45			119
46			121
47			123
48			125
49			127
50			129

THE BOOK CLUB BOOK JOURNAL

#1. Title:

Author: ....

Publisher: ....

Fiction: ◯　　　　Non-Fiction: ◯

Genre / Subject: ....

Chosen by: ....

Reviews:

....
....
....
....
....
....
....
....
....
....
....
....

Star Rating:

#2. Title:

Author: ....

Publisher: ....

Fiction: ◯   Non-Fiction: ◯

Genre / Subject: ....

Chosen by: ....

Reviews:

....
....
....
....
....
....
....
....
....
....
....
....
....

Star Rating:

THE BOOK CLUB BOOK JOURNAL

#3. Title:

Author: ....

Publisher: ....

Fiction: ◯   Non-Fiction: ◯

Genre / Subject: ....

Chosen by: ....

Reviews:

....
....
....
....
....
....
....
....
....
....
....
....
....

Star Rating:

#4. Title:

Author: ....

Publisher: ....

Fiction: ○   Non-Fiction: ○

Genre / Subject: ....

Chosen by: ....

Reviews:

....
....
....
....
....
....
....
....
....
....
....
....
....
....

Star Rating:

#5. Title:

Author: ....

Publisher: ....

Fiction: ◯   Non-Fiction: ◯

Genre / Subject: ....

Chosen by: ....

Review:

....
....
....
....
....
....
....
....
....
....
....
....
....

Star Rating:

#6. Title:

Author: ....

Publisher: ....

Fiction: ◯   Non-Fiction: ◯

Genre / Subject: ....

Chosen by: ....

Reviews:

....
....
....
....
....
....
....
....
....
....
....
....
....

Star Rating:

#7. Title:

Author: ....

Publisher: ....

Fiction: ◯   Non-Fiction: ◯

Genre / Subject: ....

Chosen by: ....

Reviews:

....
....
....
....
....
....
....
....
....
....
....
....
....
....

Star Rating:

#8. Title:

Author: ....

Publisher: ....

Fiction: ◯   Non-Fiction: ◯

Genre / Subject: ....

Chosen by: ....

Reviews:

....
....
....
....
....
....
....
....
....
....
....
....
....
....

Star Rating:

| #9. Title: |

Author: ....

Publisher: ....

Fiction: ⃝   Non-Fiction: ⃝

Genre / Subject: ....

Chosen by: ....

Reviews:

....
....
....
....
....
....
....
....
....
....
....
....

Star Rating:

#10. Title:

Author: ....

Publisher: ....

Fiction: ◯   Non-Fiction: ◯

Genre / Subject: ....

Chosen by: ....

Reviews:

....
....
....
....
....
....
....
....
....
....
....
....
....

Star Rating:

#11. Title:

Author: ....

Publisher: ....

Fiction: ◯   Non-Fiction: ◯

Genre / Subject: ....

Chosen by: ....

Reviews:

....
....
....
....
....
....
....
....
....
....
....
....
....

Star Rating:

#12. Title:

Author: ....

Publisher: ....

Fiction: ◯   Non-Fiction: ◯

Genre / Subject: ....

Chosen by: ....

Reviews:

....
....
....
....
....
....
....
....
....
....
....
....
....

Star Rating: ☆☆☆☆☆

#13. Title:

Author: ....

Publisher: ....

Fiction: ◯   Non-Fiction: ◯

Genre / Subject: ....

Chosen by: ....

Reviews:

....
....
....
....
....
....
....
....
....
....
....
....
....

Star Rating:

#14. Title:

Author: ....

Publisher: ....

Fiction: ◯   Non-Fiction: ◯

Genre / Subject: ....

Chosen by: ....

Reviews:

....
....
....
....
....
....
....
....
....
....
....
....
....

Star Rating:

#15. Title:

Author: ....

Publisher: ....

Fiction: ⃝   Non-Fiction: ⃝

Genre / Subject: ....

Chosen by: ....

Reviews:

....
....
....
....
....
....
....
....
....
....
....
....
....

Star Rating:

| #16. Title: |

Author: ....

Publisher: ....

Fiction: ⭕   Non-Fiction: ⭕

Genre / Subject: ....

Chosen by: ....

Reviews:

....
....
....
....
....
....
....
....
....
....
....
....
....
....

Star Rating:

#17. Title: ....

Author: ....

Publisher: ....

Fiction: ○   Non-Fiction: ○

Genre / Subject: ....

Chosen by: ....

Reviews:

....
....
....
....
....
....
....
....
....
....
....
....
....
....

Star Rating:

#18. Title:

Author: ....

Publisher: ....

Fiction: ◯   Non-Fiction: ◯

Genre / Subject: ....

Chosen by: ....

Reviews:

....
....
....
....
....
....
....
....
....
....
....
....
....

Star Rating:

#19. Title:

Author: ....

Publisher: ....

Fiction: ◯   Non-Fiction: ◯

Genre / Subject: ....

Chosen by: ....

Reviews:

....
....
....
....
....
....
....
....
....
....
....
....
....
....

Star Rating: ☆☆☆☆☆

#20. Title:

Author: ....

Publisher: ....

Fiction: ⭘   Non-Fiction: ⭘

Genre / Subject: ....

Chosen by: ....

Reviews:

....
....
....
....
....
....
....
....
....
....
....
....
....

Star Rating: ☆☆☆☆☆

#21. Title:

Author: ....

Publisher: ....

Fiction: ◯   Non-Fiction: ◯

Genre / Subject: ....

Chosen by: ....

Reviews:
....
....
....
....
....
....
....
....
....
....
....
....

Star Rating:

THE BOOK CLUB BOOK JOURNAL

#22. Title:

Author: ....

Publisher: ....

Fiction: ◯   Non-Fiction: ◯

Genre / Subject: ....

Chosen by: ....

Reviews:
....
....
....
....
....
....
....
....
....
....
....
....
....
....

Star Rating:

| #23. Title: |

Author: ....

Publisher: ....

Fiction: ◯   Non-Fiction: ◯

Genre / Subject: ....

Chosen by: ....

Reviews:

....
....
....
....
....
....
....
....
....
....
....
....
....

Star Rating:

#24. Title:

Author: ....

Publisher: ....

Fiction: ◯   Non-Fiction: ◯

Genre / Subject: ....

Chosen by: ....

Reviews:

....
....
....
....
....
....
....
....
....
....
....
....

Star Rating:

#25. Title:

Author: ....

Publisher: ....

Fiction: ◯   Non-Fiction: ◯

Genre / Subject: ....

Chosen by: ....

Review:

....
....
....
....
....
....
....
....
....
....
....
....
....

Star Rating:

#26. Title:

Author: ....

Publisher: ....

Fiction: ◯   Non-Fiction: ◯

Genre / Subject: ....

Chosen by: ....

Reviews:

....
....
....
....
....
....
....
....
....
....
....
....

Star Rating:

#27. Title:

Author: ....

Publisher: ....

Fiction: ○   Non-Fiction: ○

Genre / Subject: ....

Chosen by: ....

Reviews:
....
....
....
....
....
....
....
....
....
....
....
....

Star Rating:

THE BOOK CLUB BOOK JOURNAL

#28. Title:

Author: ....

Publisher: ....

Fiction: ⃝   Non-Fiction: ⃝

Genre / Subject: ....

Chosen by: ....

Reviews:

....
....
....
....
....
....
....
....
....
....
....
....
....

Star Rating:

#29. Title: ....

Author: ....

Publisher: ....

Fiction: ◯   Non-Fiction: ◯

Genre / Subject: ....

Chosen by: ....

Reviews:
....
....
....
....
....
....
....
....
....
....
....
....
....

Star Rating:

THE BOOK CLUB BOOK JOURNAL

#30. Title:

Author: ....

Publisher: ....

Fiction: ○   Non-Fiction: ○

Genre / Subject: ....

Chosen by: ....

Reviews:

....
....
....
....
....
....
....
....
....
....
....
....
....

Star Rating:

THE BOOK CLUB BOOK JOURNAL

#31. Title:

Author: ....

Publisher: ....

Fiction: ⃝   Non-Fiction: ⃝

Genre / Subject: ....

Chosen by: ....

Reviews:
....
....
....
....
....
....
....
....
....
....
....
....

Star Rating:

THE BOOK CLUB BOOK JOURNAL

#32. Title:

Author: ....

Publisher: ....

Fiction: ◯   Non-Fiction: ◯

Genre / Subject: ....

Chosen by: ....

Reviews:
....
....
....
....
....
....
....
....
....
....
....
....
....

Star Rating:

93

#33. Title:

Author: ....

Publisher: ....

Fiction: ◯   Non-Fiction: ◯

Genre / Subject: ....

Chosen by: ....

Reviews:

....
....
....
....
....
....
....
....
....
....
....
....
....

Star Rating:

#34. Title:

Author: ....

Publisher: ....

Fiction: ◯   Non-Fiction: ◯

Genre / Subject: ....

Chosen by: ....

Reviews:

....
....
....
....
....
....
....
....
....
....
....
....

Star Rating:

THE BOOK CLUB BOOK JOURNAL

#35. Title:

Author: ....

Publisher: ....

Fiction: ◯   Non-Fiction: ◯

Genre / Subject: ....

Chosen by: ....

Reviews:
....
....
....
....
....
....
....
....
....
....
....
....

Star Rating:

THE BOOK CLUB BOOK JOURNAL

#36. Title:

Author: ....

Publisher: ....

Fiction: ⭘   Non-Fiction: ⭘

Genre / Subject: ....

Chosen by: ....

Reviews:

....
....
....
....
....
....
....
....
....
....
....
....
....
....

Star Rating:

#37. Title:

Author: ....

Publisher: ....

Fiction: ◯   Non-Fiction: ◯

Genre / Subject: ....

Chosen by: ....

Reviews:

....
....
....
....
....
....
....
....
....
....
....
....
....

Star Rating:

| #38. Title: |

Author: ....

Publisher: ....

Fiction: ◯   Non-Fiction: ◯

Genre / Subject: ....

Chosen by: ....

Reviews:

....
....
....
....
....
....
....
....
....
....
....
....
....
....

Star Rating:

#39. Title:

Author: ....

Publisher: ....

Fiction: ◯   Non-Fiction: ◯

Genre / Subject: ....

Chosen by: ....

Reviews:
....
....
....
....
....
....
....
....
....
....
....
....
....

Star Rating:

#40. Title:

Author: ....

Publisher: ....

Fiction: ◯   Non-Fiction: ◯

Genre / Subject: ....

Chosen by: ....

Review:

....
....
....
....
....
....
....
....
....
....
....
....

Star Rating:

#41. Title:

Author: ....

Publisher: ....

Fiction: ◯   Non-Fiction: ◯

Genre / Subject: ....

Chosen by: ....

Reviews:

....
....
....
....
....
....
....
....
....
....
....
....
....

Star Rating:

THE BOOK CLUB BOOK JOURNAL

#42. Title:

Author: ....

Publisher: ....

Fiction: ◯   Non-Fiction: ◯

Genre / Subject: ....

Chosen by: ....

Reviews:
....
....
....
....
....
....
....
....
....
....
....
....

Star Rating:

#43. Title:

Author: ....

Publisher: ....

Fiction: ◯   Non-Fiction: ◯

Genre / Subject: ....

Chosen by: ....

Reviews:

....
....
....
....
....
....
....
....
....
....
....
....

Star Rating:

#44. Title:

Author: ....

Publisher: ....

Fiction: ◯   Non-Fiction: ◯

Genre / Subject: ....

Chosen by: ....

Reviews:

....
....
....
....
....
....
....
....
....
....
....
....
....

Star Rating:

#45. Title:

Author: ....

Publisher: ....

Fiction: ◯   Non-Fiction: ◯

Genre / Subject: ....

Chosen by: ....

Reviews:

....
....
....
....
....
....
....
....
....
....
....
....
....
....

Star Rating:

#46. Title:

Author: ....

Publisher: ....

Fiction: ◯   Non-Fiction: ◯

Genre / Subject: ....

Chosen by: ....

Reviews:

....
....
....
....
....
....
....
....
....
....
....
....
....

Star Rating:

#47. Title:

Author: ....

Publisher: ....

Fiction: ◯   Non-Fiction: ◯

Genre / Subject: ....

Chosen by: ....

Reviews:

....
....
....
....
....
....
....
....
....
....
....
....
....

Star Rating:

#48. Title:

Author: ....

Publisher: ....

Fiction: ○   Non-Fiction: ○

Genre / Subject: ....

Chosen by: ....

Reviews:

....
....
....
....
....
....
....
....
....
....
....
....
....
....

Star Rating:

#49. Title:

Author: ....

Publisher: ....

Fiction: ⭕   Non-Fiction: ⭕

Genre / Subject: ....

Chosen by: ....

Reviews:

....
....
....
....
....
....
....
....
....
....
....
....

Star Rating:

#50. Title:

Author: ....

Publisher: ....

Fiction: ◯   Non-Fiction: ◯

Genre / Subject: ....

Chosen by: ....

Reviews:

....
....
....
....
....
....
....
....
....
....
....
....
....

Star Rating:

Notes

Notes

Notes

About the Author

SL Beaumont was born and raised in beautiful New Zealand. Her award winning young adult series, *The Carlswick Mysteries,* is available from all good online bookstores. She graduated from the University of Otago, and has worked as a chartered accountant in Auckland, London and New York. When she's not writing, she loves to read and travel. *www.slbeaumont.com*

Made in the USA
Columbia, SC
08 November 2018